The Sayings of
Robert Louis Stevenson

The Sayings of

ROBERT LOUIS
STEVENSON

edited by

Karen Steele

Duckworth

First published in 1994 by
Gerald Duckworth & Co. Ltd.
The Old Piano Factory
48 Hoxton Square, London N1 6PB
Tel: 071 729 5986
Fax: 071 729 0015

A catalogue record for this book is available
from the British Library

ISBN 0 7156 2613 2

Typeset by Ray Davies
Printed in Great Britain by
Redwood Books, Trowbridge

Contents

To my daughters Carolyne, Nicola and Jenny
for their tolerant and supportive love.

Introduction

Robert Louis was born in Edinburgh on 13 November 1850 into the Stevenson family of lighthouse fame. He was a much loved only child brought up in an atmosphere of strong Calvinistic beliefs. These were elaborated by his nurse Alison Cunningham, who fed him bed-time tales of hell-fire and damnation which gave him hideous nightmares.

He described himself as a 'pious, snivelling, goody child' much haunted by the terrors of evil, which aroused his curiosity by their very condemnation.

After a childhood plagued with illness, and very little formal education, he studied engineering at Edinburgh University. It was taken for granted that he would follow on in the family business. But his student days were rebellious. To his parents' dismay, religion and politics came under fire as he fought against the restrictions of conventional society, preferring the world of dubious drinking establishments and the company of prostitutes and others of questionable character. He remembered later in life that he 'was a particularly brave boy ... and plunged into adventures and experiments, and ran risks' that it still surprised him to recall.

At 21 he announced that he wished to be a writer. His father, perhaps realising that his health was not ideal for the life of a lighthouse engineer, and yet hardly believing that a literary career would be financially rewarding, reluctantly agreed, as long as he studied law. Illness continued to plague him as he stretched his strength to the limit until the pressures of study and parental cossetting showed the strain. At the age of 23 his illness was deemed to be consumption and he was ordered to the south of France by his physician Dr Andrew Clark. For the first time he knew what it was like to be on the move unhampered by the presence of his parents: 'no baggage, there was the secret of existence.'

In 1874 he wrote to his mother to explain his

continual absence from home. 'You must understand that I shall be a nomad, more or less, until my days are done.' After being called to the Scottish Bar in 1875, he set out again for France, spending the summer around the artists' haunts of Fontainebleau, where in an unconventional atmosphere of similar-minded people he found peace of mind. It was at Grez-sur-Loing that he met Fanny Osbourne, an American woman ten years his senior, married with two children. After a traumatic courtship, she would eventually become his wife. Much of the next two years was spent with her in Paris, but in August 1878 she shocked him by returning to America to rejoin her husband. *Travels with a Donkey in the Cevennes* came from his need to be alone with his despair and to think about his future.

Stevenson's youthful frustrations and unconventional behaviour continually tested reactions to his passionate beliefs. He poured his thoughts onto paper in a series of essays, *Virginibus Puerisque*, and the posthumously published *Lay Morals*. He continued to question the rigours and demands of religion, believing in Christianity as a way of life, holding loyalty and kindness to his fellow man above everything. He hated to hurt anyone's feelings. As a child he tried to be kind to a lame boy but was rebuffed; he felt sadness for people from whom others turned away; he once horrified his wife by accepting a cigarette from a leper, his fear of causing offence being greater than his fear of catching the disease. He always tried to take the unpleasant at face value and looked past it for something he could praise.

In August 1879 Stevenson received a telegram from Fanny and immediately left for California. Although he was extremely short of funds he asked nothing of his friends and family, who disapproved of the whole affair, and the arduous conditions in which he travelled took a severe toll on his health. He endured nine months of poverty, hardship and illness, before Fanny finally got her divorce.

After their marriage in 1880, they returned to Scotland. It was during a summer visit to Braemar that a plot developed from his step-son Lloyd's playful drawing of a map. The game grew into the well-known adventure tale *Treasure Island*. Eventually they settled in Bournemouth in a house bought for Fanny by her father-in-law. Stevenson knew that 'marriage was a shackle for life', and was bound to change his habits, but he was never happy during these years of social respectability. He spent much of the time confined to his house and sickbed writing. Tenaciously he fought against death many times, continuing to write, or dictate, sometimes by sign language, when under orders of complete rest. In 1879 he wrote to his friend Edmund Gosse: 'According to all rule, that should have been my death; but after a while my spirit got up again in a divine frenzy, and has since kicked and spurred my vile body forward with great emphasis and success.'

Since the terror of his childhood nights, Stevenson had been fascinated by the dark side of man's nature and battled to understand the conflict between good and evil. In his essay 'Chapter on Dreams' in *Further Memories* he explains how he eventually brought his visions under control. The dreams were acted out 'by the little people who manage man's internal theatre', his 'Brownies', who shaped and moulded them into publishable tales. From one such vision came the plot of *The Strange Case of Dr Jekyll and Mr Hyde*. His step-son recorded the remarkable literary feat of this tale. In just three days Stevenson wrote the first draft of 30,000 words followed by a feverish rewrite over the following three days. On publication in 1886, it gained instant popularity, especially in America.

In 1887, after his father's death gave him some financial independence, Stevenson left England for America with his wife, step-son and mother. On his arrival in New York he was greeted with unexpected fame and unwelcome attention from the press. After wintering at Lake Saranac they travelled to California to join Fanny, who had gone ahead and had chartered the yacht *Casco* to cruise in the South Seas.

After two years' wandering he knew that if he returned home he would die. The Pacific climate suited him and, having bought a piece of land in Samoa, he decided to settle there. He missed Scotland and his friends, and begged them to visit. Sidney Colvin, William Henley, Edmund Gosse, Henry James, Charles

Baxter were essential to him for companionship, amusement, consolation. When he was away he had to receive letters. He needed the voices that complained and demanded, and in exile his correspondence was a life-line. To Henley, in 1884, he wrote a desperate letter with large print scribbled across the page: 'IF NOBODY WRITES TO ME I SHALL DIE.'

Stevenson's prolific correspondence (2,800 letters survive) was his only outlet during bouts of depression and despair. The letters reveal a man of great warmth, humour and eccentricity. He had a compassionate understanding of failure in others; he would fight for the under-dog, support lost causes and oppose injustice. His charm was universally attractive. He had a sparkling wit and the ability to enjoy what life had to offer. According to Sidney Colvin his eyes held 'a steady, penetrating fire' which captured the attention of everyone in his company.

The responsibility of caring for a family that included Fanny's own children and the retainers and workers at their Samoan home, Vailima, which he had had to build, and his generosity to friends drained his resources to the limit. Money was the driving force behind his work. Novels, essays, poems, short stories poured from him.

In Samoa Stevenson's life took on a new dimension. He was strong and healthy enough to enjoy to the full the role of patriach and plantation owner, and to be able to ride, swim, walk, and to give and attend parties. His death at 44 was unexpected, for he had been in good health for some time. He had spent the day catching up with his correspondence and working on chapter nine of *The Weir of Hermiston*, breaking off with the words, 'It seemed unprovoked, a wilful convulsion of brute nature …' This was descriptive of the cerebral haemorrhage that brought him to his knees on that evening of 3 December 1894, while he was helping his wife prepare dinner. He died shortly afterwards.

Though he had written 'in my heart of hearts I long to be buried among good Scots clods', his final wish was that he should be laid to rest in the country that had given him four years of healthy living. He was buried on the top of Mount Vaea behind his house. There, 1,300

feet above the only home he ever owned, his slender
body was laid in a tomb, engraved with his own epitaph:

> Under the wide and starry sky,
> Dig the grave and let me lie.
> Glad did I live and gladly die,
> And I laid me down with a will.
> This be the verse you grave for me
> Here he lies where he longed to be
> Home is the sailor home from the sea
> And the hunter home from the hill.

The grave is still lovingly cared for by the Samoans,
who call him 'Tusitala', Teller of Tales.

Robert Louis Stevenson did not approve of using too
many adjectives, but many have been employed to draw
his picture. His close friend Edmund Gosse wondered
how he could 'render in words a faint impression of the
most inspiriting, the most fascinating human being that I
have known'. Stevenson always holds the reader's
attention whether in his children's stories, his tales of
adventure, his poems of love or his treatises on life.

To compose the biography of a man as elusive as
Robert Louis Stevenson is difficult enough. To capture
the essence of his thoughts in his most characteristic and
enduring utterances no easier, but I hope that this
collection will go some way towards fulfilling that
worthwhile task.

Sources

Stevenson's main publications, with original dates, were as follows:

1879	*Picturesque Notes on Edinburgh*
	Travels with a Donkey in the Cevennes
1881	*Virginibus Puerisque*
1882	*Familiar Studies of Men & Books*
	Treasure Island
	New Arabian Nights
1885	*Prince Otto*
	The Child's Garden of Verses
	More New Arabian Nights
1886	*The Strange Case of Dr Jekyll & Mr Hyde*
	Kidnapped
1887	*Underwoods*
	Memories & Portraits
1888	*The Black Arrow*
	The Wrong Box (with Lloyd Osbourne)
1889	*The Master of Ballantrae*
1890	*In the South Seas*
1892	*The Wrecker* (with Lloyd Osbourne)
1893	*Catriona* (a sequel to *Kidnapped*)

The limited 'Edinburgh edition' of 1894-98 collected a number of unprinted pieces. Most quotations, however, have been taken from the 'Tusitala edition' published in many octavo volumes by Heinemann in the 1920s and are so referred to under title, as follows:

Amateur Emigrant, vol. 18
Essays Literary & Critical, vol. 28
Ethical Studies, vol. 26
Fables and Other Stories and Fragments, vol. 5
Familiar Studies of Men & Books, vol. 27
Footnote to History, vol. 21
Further Memories, vol. 30
Inland Voyage, vol. 17
In the South Seas, vol. 20
Memories & Portraits, vol. 29
New Arabian Nights, vol. 1
The Strange Case of Dr Jekyll & Mr Hyde, vol. 5
Travels with a Donkey in the Cevennes, vol. 17
Vailima Papers, vol. 21
Virginibus Puerisque, vol. 25

The Wrecker, vol. 12

Poetical extracts are taken from:
Poems, vol. 1, Tusitala, vol. 22
Poems, vol. 2, Tusitala, vol. 23
Collected Poems, edited by Janet Adam Smith, Hart Davis, 1950

Extracts from letters, given by recipient and date, are in
Tusitala vols 31-35 or *Stevenson's Letters to Charles Baxter* edited
by Ferguson & Waingrow (1956)

Other sources:
An Old Song and Edifying Letters of the Rutherford Family edited
    by Roger C. Swearingen (1982)
With Stevenson in Samoa by Henry Moors (1910)
An Intimate Portrait of Robert Louis Stevenson by Lloyd Osbourne
    (1924)

Childhood & Parents

The pleasant land of counterpane.

A Child's Garden of Verses

                  … fairyland,
Where all the children dine at five,
And all the playthings come alive.

ibid.

In winter I get up at night
And dress by yellow candle-light
In summer, quite the other way,
I have to go to bed by day.

ibid.

A child should always say what's true
And speak when it is spoken to,
And behave mannerly at table;
At least as far as he is able.

ibid.

When I am grown to man's estate
I shall be very proud and great,
And tell the other girls and boys
Not to meddle with my toys.

ibid.

In the child's world of dim sensation, play is all in all.
'Making believe' is the gist of his whole life, and he
cannot so much as take a walk except in character.

Virginibus Puerisque, 'Child's play'

… although the ways of children cross with those of
their elders in a hundred places daily, they never go in
the same direction nor so much as lie in the same
element.

ibid.

For none more than children are concerned for beauty
and, above all, for beauty in the old.

Memories & Portraits, 'The manse'

From the mind of childhood there is more history and more philosophy to be fished up than from all the printed volumes in a library.

Further Memories, 'Rosa quo locorum'

Children are certainly too good to be true.

to Mrs Sitwell, Jan. 1874

I have discovered why I get on always so ill, am always so nasty, so much worse than myself, with my parents; it is because they always take me at my worst, seek out my faults, and never give me any credit.

to Mrs Sitwell, Nov. 1874

I have such a longing for children of my own; and yet I do not think I could bear it if I had one.

to Mrs Sitwell, Jan. 1875

I think most people exaggerate the capacity for happiness in a child.

Memories & Portraits, 'Memoirs of himself'

The idea of sin, attached to particular actions absolutely, far from repelling, soon exerts an attraction on young minds.   *ibid.*

Succeed in frightening a child and he takes refuge in duplicity.   *Footnote to History*, ch. 3

A first child is a rival, but a second is only a rival to the first.   to Edmund Gosse, July 1879

... perhaps, after all, it is better that the lad should break his neck than that you should break his spirit.

Amateur Emigrant, 'Early impressions'

To speak truth there must be moral equality or else no respect; and hence between parent and child intercourse is apt to degenerate into a verbal fencing-bout, and misapprehensions to become ingrained.

Virginibus Puerisque, pt. 4

A father must surely rank very low and feel with great bitterness, if he finds himself in the Kingdom of Heaven and all his offspring elsewhere.

Edifying Letters of the Rutherford Family, Letter 1

The love of parents for their children is, of all natural affections, the most ill-starred ... Because the parent either looks for too much, or at least for something inappropriate, at his offspring's hands, it is too often insufficiently repaid.

Ethical Studies, 'Reflections and remarks on human life', pt. 2

Friends & Friendship

Desiderata
1. Good Health
2. 2 to 3 hundred a year
3. O du lieber Gott, friends! AMEN.

to Mrs Sitwell, Aug. 1874

You could read Kant by yourself, if you wanted; but you must share a joke with some one else.

Virginibus Puerisque, pt. 1

… it is only by trying to understand others that we can get our own hearts understood.

ibid., pt. 4

Give us grace and strength to forbear and to persevere … Spare to us our friends, soften to us our enemies.

Vailima Papers, Prayer

… no man is useless while he has a friend.

Ethical Studies, 'Lay morals', ch. 4

I had companions, I had friends
I had of whisky various blends.
The whisky was all drunk; and lo!
The friends were gone for evermo!

to W.E. Henley, Mar. 1884

When I was sick and safe in gaol
I thought my friends would never fail.
One wrote me nothing; t'other bard
Sent me an insolent post card.

ibid.

It's an owercome sooth for age an' youth
And it brooks wi' nae denial,
That the dearest friends are the auldest friends
And the young are just on trial.

Poems, vol. 1, 'Underwoods', bk. 2

Neither time nor space nor enmity can conquer old
affection.

Amateur Emigrant, Dedication to R.A.M Stevenson

The powers and the grounds of friendship are a mystery.

Memories & Portraits, 'Old mortality', pt. 3

Most men, when they repent, oblige their friends to
share the bitterness of that repentance.

ibid.

A violent friend, a brimstone enemy, is always either
loathed or slavishly adored; indifference impossible.

to James Barrie, Apr. 1893

Happiness & Pleasure

… a man is never martyred in any honest sense in the pursuit of his pleasure.   to Edmund Gosse, Jan. 1886

Every one who is happy desires to sing, whether or not they be able.
Silverado Squatters, 'Silverado diary' 23.5.80

A nice point in human history falls to be decided by Californian and Australian wines.   *ibid.*, 'Napa wine'

The world is so full of a number of things
I'm sure we should all be as happy as kings.
A Child's Garden of Verses

Nothing like a little judicious levity.
The Wrecker, ch. 7

The sight of a pleasure in which we cannot or else will not share moves us to a particular impatience.
Ethical Studies, 'Christmas sermon', pt. 2

… as we go on in years, we are all tempted to frown upon our neighbour's pleasures.   *ibid.*

In his own life, then, a man is not to expect happiness, only to profit by it gladly when it shall arise.
ibid., pt. 3

There is no duty we so much underrate as the duty of being happy.
Virginibus Puerisque, 'An apology for idlers'

By being happy, we sow anonymous benefits upon the world, which remain unknown even to ourselves or, when they are disclosed, surprise nobody so much as the benefactor.   *ibid.*

Pleasures are more beneficial than duties because, like the quality of mercy, they are not strained, and they are twice blest.   *ibid.*

A happy man or woman is a better thing to find than a five pound note.   *ibid.*

Total abstinence, like all ascetical conclusions, is unfriendly to the most generous, cheerful and human parts of man ...   *Amateur Emigrant*, 'Steerage types'

... I do not like to think of a life without the red wine on the table and the tobacco with its lovely little coal of fire.
to Henry James, June 1893

The only reason a wise man can assign for getting drunk is that he wishes to enjoy for a while the blessed immunities and sunshiny weather of the land of fooldom.   to Charles Baxter, Oct. 1872

To draw a life without delights is to prove I have not realised it.   *Further Memories*, 'Lantern bearers', pt. 2

... the ground of a man's joy is often hard to hit.
ibid., pt. 3

I wish that life were an opera. I should like to live in one; but I don't know in what quarter of the globe I shall find a society so constituted.
to Mrs Thomas Stevenson, Aug. 1872

To see people skipping all round us with their eyes sealed up with indifference, knowing nothing of the earth or man or woman, going automatically to offices and saying they are happy or unhappy – out of a sense of duty, I suppose, surely at least from no sense of happiness or unhappiness ...
to Mrs Sitwell, Autumn 1874

Many's the long night I've dreamed of cheese – toasted, mostly.   *Treasure Island*, ch. 15

Hope, Faith & Religion

Hope, they say, deserts us at no period of our existence.
Virginibus Puerisque, pt. 2

From first to last, and in the face of smarting disillusions, we continue to expect good fortune, better health, and better conduct; and that so confidently, that we judge it needless to deserve them. *ibid.*

Every sin is our last; every 1st of January a remarkable turning-point in our career.
ibid.

There is always a new horizon for onward-looking men.
Virginibus Puerisque, 'El Dorado'

An aspiration is a joy for ever, a possession as solid as a landed estate, a fortune which we can never exhaust and which gives us year by year a revenue of pleasurable activity. *ibid.*

Happily we all shoot at the moon with ineffectual arrows; our hopes are set on inaccessible El Dorado; we come to an end of nothing here below.
ibid.

The soul of piety was killed long ago by that idea of reward.
to Edmund Gosse, Jan. 1886

Faith means holding the same opinions as the person employing the word.
Memories & Portraits, 'From his notebook'

Christ was always such a great gentleman; you can always count on His doing the right thing ...
New Arabian Nights, Introduction

Think a little more of other people's souls and less of your own. I am sure Christ never intended you to concentrate all your thoughts on yourself.

ibid.

... is there anything in life so disenchanting as attainment?

ibid., 'Adventure of the hansom cabs'

The worst of our education is that Christianity does not recognise and hallow Sex.

to R.A.M Stevenson, Sept. 1894

How is it that men only believe in God when they are in trouble?

With Stevenson in Samoa, ch. 4

If you are sure that God, in the long run, means kindness by you, you should be happy; and if happy surely you should be kind.

to Mrs Thomas Stevenson, Dec. 1880

... the faithful desire to do right is accepted by God: that seems to me to be the gospel, and that was how Christ delivered us from the law.   *ibid.*

Faith is, not to believe the Bible, but to believe in God.

ibid.

There are only three possible attitudes; Optimism, which has gone to smash: Pessimism, which is on the rising hand and very popular among clergymen who seem to think they are Christians ... and this Faith, which is the gospel.   *ibid.*

The Bible, in most parts, is a cheerful book; it is our little piping theologies, tracts and sermons that are dull and dowie.   to Mr Dick, March 1884

We may learn a great deal about religion, yet not learn religion.

Vailima Papers, 'Address to Samoan students'

The meaning of religion is a rule of life; it is an obligation to do well ...

ibid.

We are all like St Paul in this, that we see better things than we are able to attain to.

ibid.

We cannot ... hope to be seen doing what we teach, but we must be seen trying to do it.

ibid.

Can it be that the Puritan school, by ... setting a stamp of its disapproval on whole fields of human activity and interest, leads at last directly to material greed.

Amateur Emigrant, 'Steerage types'

Most men, finding themselves the authors of their own disgrace, rail the louder against God or destiny.

Memories & Portraits, 'Old mortality', pt. 3

God will make good to you all the good you have done, and mercifully forgive you all your evil.

to Alison Cunningham, 1871

We are not damned for doing wrong, but for not doing right ...

Ethical Studies, 'Christmas sermon', pt. 1

There goes another Faithful Failure.

ibid., pt. 4

The Gods are dead. Perhaps they are. God knows.

Collected Poems, 'Light verse'

It's strange that God should fash to frame
The yearth and lift sae hie,
An' clean forget to explain the same
To a gentleman like me.

Poems, vol. 1, 'Underwoods', bk. 2

If I could arise and travel away
Over the plains of the night and the day,
I should arrive at a land at last
Where all of our sins and sorrows are past
And we're done with the ten commandments.

Poems, vol. 2, 'New poems'

Shut your eyes hard against the recollection of your sins.
Do not be afraid, you will not be able to forget them.

Ethical Studies, 'Reflections and remarks on human life', pt. 7

Human Nature

... what one wants to know is not what people did, but why they did it, or rather why they thought they did it; and to learn that, you should go to the men themselves. Their very falsehood is often more than another man's truth.

to Maud Babington, Summer 1871

There is a sort of dead-alive, hackneyed people about, who are scarcely conscious of living except in the exercise of some conventional occupation.

Virginibus Puerisque, 'An apology for idlers'

It is only by trying to understand others that we can get our own hearts understood.

Virginibus Puerisque, pt. 4

It is much more important to do right than not to do wrong; further, the one is possible, the other has always been and will ever be impossible.

to Mrs Thomas Stevenson, Dec. 1880

In moments of effort, one learns to do the easy things that people like.

to Edmund Gosse, Mar. 1884

There is a wonderful callousness in human nature which enables us to live.

to Edmund Gosse, Oct. 1879

It is the history of our kindnesses that alone makes this world tolerable.

to Edmund Gosse, Nov. 1879

You cannot run away from a weakness; you must some time fight it out or perish.

Amateur Emigrant, 'Steerage types'

… the dirtier people are in their persons the more delicate is their sense of modesty.

ibid., 'Despised races'

Pathos must be relieved by dignity of treatment.

ibid., 'The emigrant train'

The imagination loves to trifle with what is not.

Silverado Squatters, 'Sea fogs'

The true Bohemian … lives wholly to himself, does what he wishes, and not what is thought proper, buys what he wants for himself and not what is thought proper, works at what he believes he can do well and not what will bring him in money or favour.

Ethical Studies, 'Lay morals', ch. 4

Everyone lives by selling something, whatever be his right to it.

Virginibus Puerisque, 'Beggars'

To a man in an abject situation, a good twanging snarl is a sort of moral pinch of snuff, and pulls his nerves together.

An Old Song, ch. 8

I regard you with an indifference closely bordering on aversion.

New Arabian Nights, 'Rajah's diamond Bandbox'

Superstitions outlast their utility like street lamps burning on into the daylight.

Edifying Letters of the Rutherford Family, Letter 1

Justice is not done to the versatility and the unplumbed childishness of man's imagination.

Further Memories, 'Lantern bearers', pt. 2

I do not care two straws for all the nots.

Ethical Studies, 'Reflections and remarks on human life', pt. 4

Never allow your mind to dwell on your own misconduct; that is ruin.

ibid., pt. 7

The conscience has morbid sensibilities; it must be employed but not indulged ...

ibid.

You will always do wrong: you must try to get used to that, my son.

ibid.

Courage is the principal virtue, for all the others presuppose it.

ibid., pt. 12

Strange are the ways of men
And strange the ways of God!
We tread the mazy paths
That all our fathers trod.

Poems, vol. 2, 'New poems'

Knowledge, Learning & Conversation

The great thing is to know as much science as your mind will stand without turning into a man of science.

to Garrett Droppers, Apr. 1887

Know as much of the world as your heart will bear without your turning into a man of the world.

ibid.

In a great measure our power of thinking is limited by our knowledge of words.

Memories & Portraits, 'From his notebook'

I never know whether to be more surprised at Darwin himself for making so much of Natural Selection, or at his opponents for making so little of it.

ibid.

He who makes a study of character seeks to learn the commonplaces of the period, the catch-words and shibboleths, the established decencies of thought and speech and conduct, in order that he may set them aside and see the man himself.

ibid.

Scientific men, who imagine that their science affords an answer to the problems of existence, are perhaps the most to be pitied of mankind; and contemned.

ibid.

We cannot ... hope to be seen doing what we teach, but we must be seen trying to do it.

Vailima Papers, 'Address to Samoan students'

The first step for all is to learn to the dregs our own ignoble fallibility.

Memories & Portraits, 'Old mortality', pt. 2

The problem of education is twofold: first to know, and then to utter.

Ethical Studies, 'Lay morals', ch. 1

Every generation has to educate another which it has brought upon the stage.

ibid.

The speaker buries his meaning; it is for the hearer to dig it up again; and all speech, written or spoken, is in a dead language until it finds a willing and prepared hearer.   *ibid.*

Education, as practised, is a form of harnessing with the friendliest intentions.

Essays Literary & Critical, 'On the choice of a profession'

Every man should learn what is within him, that he may strive to mend; he must be taught what is without him, that he may be kind to others.

ibid., 'The morality of the profession of letters'

… it can never be safe to suppress what is true.

ibid.

There is nothing more disenchanting to man than to be shown the springs and mechanism of any art … .

ibid., 'On some technical elements of style in literature'

Passion, wisdom, creative force, the power of mystery or colour, are allotted in the hour of birth, and can be neither learned nor simulated.

ibid., 'A note on realism'

How small a thing creates an immortality!

Further Memories, 'Coast of Fife'

History is much decried; it is a tissue of errors, we are told, no doubt correctly; and rival historians expose each other's blunders with gratification.

Ethical Studies, 'The day after tomorrow'

A good talk is not to be had for the asking.
Memories & Portraits, 'Talk and talkers', pt. 1

... the excitement of a good talk lives for a long while after in the blood, the heart still hot within you, the brain still simmering, and the physical earth swimming around you with the colours of the sun.

ibid.

No human being ever spoke of scenery for above two minutes at a time, which makes me suspect we hear too much of it in literature.

ibid.

Talk is indeed both the scene and instrument of friendship.

ibid.

The correction of silence is what kills: when you know you have transgressed, and your friend says nothing and avoids your eye.

ibid., pt. 2

To the old our mouths are always partly closed; we must swallow our obvious retorts and listen.

ibid.

The old appear in conversation in two characters: the critically silent and the garrulous anecdotic.   *ibid.*

The cruellest lies are often told in silence.
Virginibus Puerisque, pt. 4

The talk of a workman is apt to be more interesting than that of a wealthy merchant, because the thoughts, hopes, and fears of which the workman's life is built lie nearer to necessity and nature.
Amateur Emigrant, 'Personal experiences and review'

It is our business here to speak, for it is by the tongue that we multiply ourselves most influentially.
Ethical Studies, 'Reflections and remarks on human life', pt. 4

To speak kindly, wisely and pleasantly is the first of duties, the easiest of duties and the duty that is most blessed in its performance.

ibid.

You will learn a great deal of virtue by studying any art; but nothing of any art in the study of virtue.

ibid., pt. 7

I cannot lead who follow - I
Who learn, am dumb to teach;
I can but indicate the goals
That greater men shall reach.

Poems, vol. 2, 'New poems'

When a man begins to sharpen one faculty, and keeps on sharpening it with tireless perseverance, he can achieve wonders.

An Intimate Portrait of RLS

Labour & Idleness

For no man can be honest who does not work.
Ethical Studies, 'Lay morals', ch. 4

To ask to see some fruit of our endeavour is but a transcendental way of serving for reward.
ibid., 'Christmas sermon', pt. 1

A man dissatisfied with his endeavours is a man tempted to sadness.
ibid., pt. 2

… if a man love the labour of any trade apart from any question of success or fame, the gods have called him.
Essays Literary & Critical, 'Letter to a young gentleman'

Nothing is perhaps more notable in the average workman than his surprising idleness, and the candour with which he confesses to the failing.
Amateur Emigrant, 'Personal experiences and review'

… the average mechanic recognises his idleness with effrontery; he has even, as I am told, organised it.
ibid.

It is not sufficiently recognised that our race detests work.
ibid.

Man is an idle animal.
Ethical Studies, 'The day after tomorrow'

Idleness which is often becoming and even wise in the bachelor, begins to wear a different aspect when you have a wife to support.
Virginibus Puerisque, pt. 2

While others are filling their memory with a lumber of words, one-half of which they will forget before the week be out, your truant may learn some really useful art: to play the fiddle, to know a good cigar, or to speak with ease and opportunity to all varieties of men.

ibid., 'An apology for idlers'

... it is not only the person himself who suffers his busy habits, but his wife and children, his friends and relations, and down to the very people he sits with in a railway carriage or an omnibus.

ibid.

Extreme busyness, whether at school or college, kirk or market, is a symptom of deficient vitality.

ibid.

Perpetual devotion to what a man calls his business, is only to be sustained by perpetual neglect of many other things.

ibid.

The dull man is made, not by the nature, but by the degree of his immersion in a single business.

The Wrecker, ch. 15

There is nothing quite useless in the world except stupidity; and even that may dance profitably enough upon the treadmill.

Edifying Letters of the Rutherford Family, Letter 1

Here lies a man who never did
Anything but what he was bid;
Who lived his life in paltry ease
And died of commonplace disease.

to Cosmo Monkhouse, March 1884

The saddest object in civilisation, and to my mind the greatest confession of its failure, is the man who can work, who wants to work, and who is not allowed to work.

An Intimate Portrait of RLS

Life & Death

Each has his own tree of ancestors, but at the top of all sits Probably Arboreal.

Memories & Portraits, 'Pastoral'

Our conscious years are but a moment in the history of the elements that build us.

ibid., 'The manse'

We don't live for the necessities of life; in reality no one cares a damn for them; what we live for are its superfluities.

An Intimate Portrait of RLS

To be honest, to be kind – to earn a little and to spend a little less, to make, upon the whole, a family happier for his presence.

Ethical Studies, 'Christmas sermon', pt. 1

An unconscionable time a-dying – there is the picture … of your life and mine.

ibid.

In his own life, then, a man is not to expect happiness, only to profit by it gladly when it shall arise.

ibid., pt. 3

Life is not designed to minister to a man's vanity.

ibid., pt. 4

Here lies one who meant well, tried a little, failed much: – surely that may be his epitaph, of which he need not be ashamed.

ibid.

To believe in immortality is one thing, but it is first needful to believe in life.

Memories & Portraits, 'Old mortality', pt. 3

No man is of any use until he has dared everything;
to Sidney Colvin, Aug. 1879

Life is not all Beer and Skittles.
to Sidney Colvin, Aug. 1893

We are all busy in this world building Towers of Babel;
Virginibus Puerisque, Introduction

Life is only a very dull and ill-directed theatre unless we have some interests in the piece.   *ibid.*, 'El Dorado'

Doubtless the world is quite right in a million ways; but you have to be kicked about a little to convince you of the fact.   *ibid.*, 'Crabbed age and youth'

It is really very disheartening how we depend on other people in this life.
Silverado Squatters, pt. 2

Life, my old shipmate, life, at any moment and in any view, is as dangerous as a sinking ship.
Fables and Other Stories and Fragments, 'The sinking ship'

There are always high and brave and amusing lives to be lived; and a change of key, however exotic, does not exclude melody.
to Mrs Charles Fairchild, Aug. 1892

Every man is his own judge and mountain-guide through life.
Ethical Studies, 'Lay morals', ch. 2

Nothing should be done in a hurry that can be done slowly.
Essays Literary & Critical, 'Morality of the profession of letters'

There is only one wish realisable on the earth; only one thing that can be perfectly attained: Death. And from a variety of circumstances we have no one to tell us whether it be worth attaining.
Virginibus Puerisque, 'El Dorado'

... it is better to be a fool than to be dead.

ibid., 'Crabbed age and youth'

... even if the doctor does not give you a year, even if he hesitates about a month, make one brave push and see what can be accomplished in a week.

ibid., 'Aes triplex'

Who would find heart enough to begin to live, if he dallied with the consideration of death.   *ibid.*

... life is a Permanent Possibility of Sensation.   *ibid.*

The world has no room for cowards. We must all be ready somehow to toil, to suffer, to die.

Vailima Papers, 'Address to Samoan students'

Cease to live I may; but not cease to be: it can only be a change of function.

Memories & Portraits, 'From his notebook'

Under the wide and starry sky,
Dig the grave and let me lie.
Glad did I live and gladly die,
And I laid me down with a will.

Poems, vol. 2, 'Underwoods', bk. 1

If I desire to live long, it is that I may have the more to look back upon.

Further Memories, 'A retrospect'

God help us all, this is a rough world ...

to Mrs Sitwell, Apr. 1874

God help us all, it is a funny world.

to Mrs Sitwell, Sept. 1874

I have trod the upward and the downward slope
I have endured and done in days before;
I have longed for all, and bid farewell to hope;
I have lived and loved, and closed the door.

Poems, vol. 1, 'Songs of travel'

Life is monstrous, infinite, illogical, abrupt and poignant;
Memories & Portraits, 'A humble remonstrance'

Life goes before us, infinite in complication.   *ibid.*

Life is far better fun than people dream who fall asleep
among the chimney stacks and telegraph wires.
to Sidney Colvin, Aug. 1889

But death is no bad friend; a few aches and gasps, and
we are done.
to Edmund Gosse, Dec. 1879

I trust also you may be long without finding out the
devil that there is in a bereavement. After love it is the
one great surprise that life preserves for us.
to Edmund Gosse, Sept. 1883

The graveyard may be cloakroom to Heaven; but we
must admit that it is a very ugly and offensive vestibule
in itself, however fair may be the life to which it leads.
Further Memories, 'Wreath of immortelles'

Though we steer after a fashion, yet we must sail
according to the winds and currents.
Ethical Studies, 'Reflections and remarks on human life', pt. 8

The look of death is both severe and mild,
And all the words of Death are grave and sweet.
Poems, vol. 2, 'New poems'

Literature

What kind of talent is required to please this mighty public? That was my first question, and was soon amended with the words, 'if any'.

Essays Literary & Critical, 'Popular authors', pt. 4

There are two duties incumbent upon any man who enters on the business of writing: truth to the fact and a good spirit in the treatment.

ibid., 'Morality of the profession of letters'

The fortune of a tale lies not alone in the skill of him that writes, but as much, perhaps, in the inherited experience of him who reads. *Memories & Portraits*, 'Pastoral'

The difficulty of literature is not to write, but to write what you mean; not to affect your reader, but to affect him precisely as you wish. *Virginibus Puerisque*, pt. 4

Books are good enough in their own way, but they are a mighty bloodless substitute for life.

ibid., 'An apology for idlers'

If I don't rewrite them it's because I don't see how to write them better, not because I don't think they should be. to W.E. Henley, Apr. 1879

How the French misuse their freedom; see nothing worth writing about save the eternal triangle; while we who are muzzled like dogs, but who are infinitely wider in our outlook, are condemned to avoid half the life that passes us by. *An Intimate Portrait of RLS*

The bourgeoisie's weapon is starvation. If as a writer or an artist you run counter to their narrow notions they simply and silently withdraw your means of subsistence.

ibid.

It bored me hellishly to write the Emigrant; well, it's going to bore others to read it; that's only fair.

to Sidney Colvin, Jan. 1880

There is but one art, to omit! O if I knew how to omit, I would ask no other knowledge.

to R.A.M. Stevenson, Oct. 1883

A man who knew how to omit would make an *Iliad* of a daily paper.   *ibid.*

I know that good work sometimes hits; but with my hand on my heart, I think it is by an accident.

to Edmund Gosse, Jan. 1886

What the public likes is work (of any kind) a little loosely executed.   *ibid.*

Fiction is to the grown man what play is to the child; it is there that he changes the atmosphere and tenor of his life.

Memories & Portraits, 'Gossip on romance'

Drama is the poetry of conduct, romance the poetry of circumstance.   *ibid.*

The life of man is not the subject of novels, but the inexhaustible magazine from which subjects are to be selected.

ibid., 'A humble remonstrance'

… if you can interest a person for an hour and a half, you have not been idle.

to John Meiklejohn, Feb. 1880

We want incident, interest, action: to the devil with your philosophy.   *ibid.*

If there is anywhere a thing said in two sentences that could have been as clearly and as engagingly and as forcibly said in one, then it's amateur work.

to William Archer, Feb. 1888

Humanly speaking, it is a more important matter to play the fiddle, even badly, than to write huge works upon recondite subjects.

Amateur Emigrant, 'Steerage scenes'

… letter writing is a terrible venture of a man's soul; … you may have changed your mind, or seen reason to feel quite coldly towards your correspondent, long before your production finds its way into his hands.

Edifying Letters of the Rutherford Family, Letter 1

I hope you don't dislike reading bad style like this as much as I do writing it; it hurts me when neither words nor clauses fall into their places, … I do feel so inclined to break the pen and write no more.

to Mrs Sitwell, Nov. 1873

If you are going to make a book end badly, it must end badly from the beginning.

to James Barrie, Nov. 1892

Love

Falling in love and winning love are often difficult tasks to overbearing and rebellious spirits:
Virginibus Puerisque, 'El Dorado'

The true love story commences at the altar, when there lies before the married pair a most beautiful contest of wisdom and generosity, and a life-long struggle towards an unattainable ideal.

ibid.

… the ideal story is that of two people who go into love step for step, with a fluttered consciousness, like a pair of children venturing together into a dark room.

ibid., pt. 3

From the first moment when they see each other, with a pang of curiosity, through stage after stage of growing pleasure and embarrassment, they can read the expression of their own trouble in each other's eyes.

ibid.

Falling in love is the one illogical adventure, the one thing of which we are tempted to think as supernatural, in our trite and reasonable world.

ibid.

There is here no declaration properly so called; the feeling is so plainly shared, that as soon as the man knows what is in his own heart, he is sure of what is in the woman's.

ibid.

Love should run out to meet love with open arms.

ibid.

The simple act of falling in love is as beneficial as it is astonishing.   *ibid.*

The lover takes a perilous pleasure in privately
displaying his weak points and having them, one after
another, accepted and condoned.

ibid.

The body is a house of many windows: there we all sit,
showing ourselves and crying on the passers-by to come
and love us.

ibid., pt. 4

... don't be too ready to believe in love: there are many
shams: the true love will not allow you to reason about it.

to Trevor Haddon, June 1882

All things on earth and sea
All that the white stars see
Turns about you and me

Poems, vol. 2, 'New poems'

The earth through all her bowers
Carols and breathes and flowers
About this love of ours.

ibid.

Let Love go, if go she will.
Seek not, O fool, her wanton flight to stay.
Of all she gives and takes away
The best remains behind her still.

ibid.

Love – what is love? A great and aching heart
Wrung hands; and silence; and a long despair.

ibid.

You do not love another because he is wealthy or wise or
eminently respectable; you love him because you love
him; that is love ...

Ethical Studies, 'Lay morals', ch. 3

So long as we love we serve; so long as we are loved by others I would almost say that we are indispensable.

ibid., ch. 4

There is nothing more becoming than a genuine admiration; and it shares this with love, that it does not become contemptible although misplaced.

Amateur Emigrant, 'Steerage scenes'

... to live out of doors with the woman a man loves is of all lives the most complete and free.

Travels with a Donkey in the Cevennes, 'A night among the pines'

Manners, Ethics & Society

The individual is more affecting than the mass.
Amateur Emigrant, 'Early impressions'

I have little of the radical in social questions, and have always nourished an idea that one person was as good as another.
ibid., 'Steerage scenes'

We are all ready to laugh at the ploughman among lords; we should consider also the case of a lord among the ploughmen.
ibid., 'Personal experiences and review'

To be a gentleman is to be one all the world over, and in every relation and grade of society.
ibid.

... manners, like art, should be human and central.
ibid.

I have often marvelled at the impudence of gentlemen who describe and pass judgment on the life of man, in almost perfect ignorance of all its necessary elements and natural careers.
The Wrecker, ch. 15

... a man's view of the universe is mostly a view of the civilised society in which he lives.
Ethical Studies, 'Lay morals', ch. 4

He has not risen by climbing himself, but by pushing others down.
Further Memories, 'The satirist'

Gentleness and cheerfulness, these come before all morality; they are the perfect duties.
Ethical Studies, 'Christmas sermon', pt. 2

Noble disappointment, noble self-denial, are not to be admired, not even to be pardoned, if they bring bitterness.   *ibid.*

If your morals make you dreary depend upon it they are wrong. I do not say 'give them up', for they may be all you have; but conceal them like a vice, lest they should spoil the lives of better and simpler people.
                                                        ibid.

... how disagreeable it is to have your private affairs and private unguarded expressions getting into print.
                                                        to Charles Baxter, May 1889

We have a butler! He doesn't buttle, but the point of the thing is the style. ... I shall have it on my tomb 'He ran a butler'.
                                                        to Sidney Colvin, Apr. 1886

I believe in the ultimate decency of things.
                                                        to Sidney Colvin, Aug. 1893

There is such a thing as loyalty to a man's own better self; and from those who have not that, God help me, how am I to look for loyalty to others.
                                                        Ethical Studies, 'Lay morals', ch. 2

The profit of every act should be this, that it was right for us to do it.   *ibid.*, ch. 3

For such things as honour and love and faith are not only nobler than food and drink, but indeed I think that we desire them more, and suffer more sharply for their absence.
                                                        New Arabian Nights, 'Lodging for the night'

... our civilisation is a hollow fraud, all the fun of life is lost by it.   to Mrs Fairchild, Sept. 1890

There's just ae thing I cannae bear,
An' that's my conscience.
                                                        Poems, vol. 2, 'Underwoods', bk. 2

An age must be measured of its own standards; seventeenth-century actions must not be tried by the moral notions of nineteenth-century enlightenment.
Memories & Portraits, 'From his notebook'

Here is a remarkable state of things in our Christian commonwealths, that the poor only should be asked to give. *Virginibus Puerisque*, 'Beggars'

It is not only our enemies, those desperate characters, it is we ourselves who know not what we do; …
Ethical Studies, 'Christmas sermon', pt. 1

That we are to suffer others to be injured, and stand by, is not conceivable, and surely not desirable.
ibid., pt. 3

… populations should not be taught to gain public ends by private crime …
to Mrs Jenkin, Apr. 1887

… for all men to bow before a threat of crime is to loosen and degrade beyond redemption the whole fabric of men's decency.
ibid.

What hangs people, my dear Pitman, is the unfortunate circumstance of guilt.
The Wrong Box, ch. 7

War is a huge entrainement.
With Stevenson in Samoa, ch. 10

It would be well if nations and races could communicate their qualities; but in practice when they look upon each other, they have an eye to nothing but defects.
Further Memories, 'Memories of Fontainebleau'

Forget wholly and forever all small pruderies and remember that you cannot change ancestral feelings of right and wrong without what is practically soul-murder.
to Adelaide Boodle, July 1894

When you seek to justify yourself to others, you may be sure you will plead falsely.

Ethical Studies, 'Reflections and remarks on human life', pt. 1

It is the business of this life to make excuses for others, but none for ourselves.

ibid.

A little society is needful to show a man his failings; for if he lives entirely by himself, he has no occasion to fall ...   *ibid.*, pt. 4

Solitude is the climax of the negative virtues.

ibid.

We ought to know distinctly that we are damned for what we do wrong; but when we have done right, we have only been gentlemen, after all.   *ibid.*, pt. 6

It is the mark of a good action that it appears inevitable in the retrospect.

ibid.

To every view of morals there are two sides: what is demanded by man; what is exacted by the conditions of life.

Ethical Studies, 'Lay morals', Introduction

The word morality is so old and so important that we begin to pay it an idolatrous adoration.

ibid., 'On morality', pt. 1

The world has no room for cowards.

Vailima Papers, 'Address to Samoan students'

Absolute uniformity of tastes in a large number of human beings is precisely the worst possible condition for peaceable coexistence;

Memories & Portraits, 'From his notebook'

Politics

We ... all know what Parliament is, and we are all ashamed of it.

Ethical Studies, 'The day after tomorrow'

There are great truths in Socialism, or no one ... would be found to hold it; and if it came, and did one-tenth part of what it offers, I for one should make it welcome.

ibid.

I am no more abashed at having been a red-hot Socialist with a panacea of my own than at having been a sucking infant ...

Virginibus Puerisque, 'Crabbed age and youth'

For my part, I look back to the time when I was a Socialist with something like regret.

ibid.

I do not greatly pride myself in having outlived my belief in the fairy tales of Socialism.

ibid.

Now I know that in thus turning Conservative with years, I am going through the normal cycle of change and travelling in the common orbit of men's opinions.

ibid.

Politics is perhaps the only profession for which no preparation is thought necessary.

Familiar Studies of Men & Books, 'Yoshida-Torajiro'

Politics is a vile and bungling business. I used to think meanly of the plumber; but he shines beside the politician!

With Stevenson in Samoa, ch. 10

Damn the political situation
    "   you
    "   me
        and
    "   Gladstone.

to Sidney Colvin, June 1886

To be politically blind is no distinction, we are all so, if you come to that.

Amateur Emigrant, 'Personal experiences and review'

I have little of the radical in social questions, and have always nourished an idea that one person was as good as another.

ibid., 'Steerage scenes'

Travel & Scotland

The first experience can never be repeated. The first love, the first sunrise, the first South Sea island, are memories apart and touched a virginity of sense.

In the South Seas, ch. 1

There is no foreign land, it is the traveller only that is foreign, and now and again, by a flash of recollection, lights up the contrasts of the earth.

Silverado Squatters, 'The return'

Sightseeing is the art of disappointment.

ibid., 'The petrified forest'

… grumbling is the traveller's pastime.

Amateur Emigrant, 'Early impressions'

This is one of the lessons of travel – that some of the strangest races dwell next door to you at home.

ibid., 'Fellow passengers'

Travel is of two kinds; and this voyage of mine across the ocean combined both … I was not only travelling out of my country in latitude and longitude, but out of myself in diet, associates, and consideration.

ibid., 'Personal experiences and review'

In America you eat better than anywhere else: fact. The food is heavenly.

to Sidney Colvin, Aug. 1879

America is … a fine place to eat in, and a great place for kindness; but, Lord, what a silly thing is popularity.

to Henry James, Sept. 1887

… the most beautiful adventures are not those we go to seek.

Inland Voyage, 'Back to the world'

And when we have discovered a continent, or crossed a chain of mountains, it is only to find another ocean or another plain upon the further side.

Virginibus Puerisque, 'El Dorado'

... to travel hopefully is a better thing than to arrive, and the true success is to labour.

ibid.

The presence of one Cockney titterer will cause a whole party to walk in clouds of darkness.

In the South Seas, ch. 2

It is this sense of kinship that the traveller must rouse and share or he had better content himself with travels from the blue bed to the brown.

ibid.

... a ship of war comes to a haven, anchors, lands party, receives and returns a visit, and the captain writes a chapter on the manners of the island.

ibid.

... anyone can stay a year in England and be the better for it, but no one can stay there steadily and not be the worse.   to Walter Simpson, Oct. 1887

Home no more home to me, whither must I wander.

to Charles Baxter, Nov. 1888

No baggage – there was the secret of existence.

The Wrecker, ch. 4

For my part, I travel not to go anywhere, but to go. I travel for travel's sake.

Travels with a Donkey in the Cevennes, 'Cheylard and Luc'

The great affair is to move; to feel the needs and hitches of our life more nearly; to come down off this feather-bed of civilisation, and find the globe granite underfoot and strewn with cutting flints.

ibid.

There is nothing under Heav'n so blue
That's fairly worth the travelling to.
Poems, vol. 1, 'Underwoods', bk. 2

You can keep no men long, nor Scotsmen at all, off
moral, or theological discussion.
Memories & Portraits, 'Talk and talkers', pt. 1

The happiest lot on earth is to be born a Scotsman.
Silverado Squatters, 'The Scot abroad'

Scotland is indefinable; it has no unity except upon the
map.   *ibid.*

And though I think I would rather die elsewhere, yet in
my heart of hearts I long to be buried among good Scots
clods.   *ibid.*

I am a Scotsman, touch me and you will find the
thistle ...   *ibid.*, 'Silverado diary'

The name of my native land is not NORTH BRITAIN
whatever may be the name of yours.
to S.R. Crockett, Spring 1888

... Edinburgh pays cruelly for her high seat in one of the
vilest climates under heaven.
Ethical Studies, 'Edinburgh: picturesque notes', ch. 1

O for ten Edinburgh minutes – sixpence between us, and
the ever-glorious Lothian Road, or dear mysterious Leith
Walk!
to Charles Baxter, Dec. 1881

Change Glenlivet for Bourbon, and it is still whisky, only
not so good.
Amateur Emigrant, 'Steerage types'

Wealth

I am like to be a millionaire if this goes on, and be publicly hanged at the social revolution: ... and it would be a godsend to my biographer, if ever I have one.

to William Archer, Oct. 1887

... an aim in life is the only fortune worth the finding; and it is not to be found in foreign lands, but in the heart itself. *Amateur Emigrant*, 'Steerage types'

There is something singularly enticing in the idea of going rent-free, into a ready-made house. *ibid.*

It is not by a man's purse, but by his character, that he is rich or poor. *ibid.*, 'Personal experiences and review'

There is more adventure in the life of the working man who descends as a common soldier into the battle of life, than in that of the millionaire who sits apart in an office ... and only directs the manoeuvres by telegraph.

ibid.

Wealth is only useful for two things: a yacht and a string quartette. *to R.A.M. Stevenson, Oct. 1887*

A thoroughly respectable income is as much as a man spends.

Essays Literary & Critical, 'Choice of a profession'

The first duty in this world is for a man to pay his way; when that is quite accomplished, he may plunge into what eccentricity he likes but emphatically not till then.

ibid., 'Letter to a young gentleman'

It is perhaps a more fortunate destiny to have a taste for collecting shells than to be born a millionaire ...

Ethical Studies, 'Lay morals', ch. 4

... it is always better policy to learn an interest than to make a thousand pounds; for the money will soon be spent ... but the interest remains imperishable and ever new. *ibid.*

To be wealthy, a rich nature is the first requisite, and money but the second. *ibid.*

The true services of life are inestimable in money, and are never paid. *ibid.*

... it will be very hard to persuade me that anyone has earned an income of a hundred thousand. *ibid.*

... what a man spends upon himself, he shall have earned by services to the race. *ibid.*

... money is not only to be spent; it has also to be earned. *ibid.*

To spendthrifts money is so living and actual – it is such a thin veil between them and their pleasures!
New Arabian Nights, 'Lodging for the night'

... a spendthrift with only a few crowns is the Emperor of Rome until they are spent. *ibid.*

A fellow has to get rid gradually of all material attachments: that was manhood, and as long as you were bound down to anything – you were still tethered by the umbilical cord. *The Wrecker*, ch. 4

... that fashion of regarding money as the means and object of existence. *In the South Seas*, ch. 2

Wealth should not be the first object of life.
Ethical Studies, 'Lay morals', Introduction

... is it not the natural motion of the soul to communicate wealth among our friends and make them all prosperous in our prosperity. *ibid.*

Women & Marriage

Women are better hearers than men, to begin with; they learn, I fear, in anguish, to bear with the tedious and infantile vanity of the other sex.

Memories & Portraits, 'Talk and talkers', pt. 2

Whatever you do, see that you don't sacrifice a woman; that's where all imperfect loves conduct us.

to Trevor Haddon, June 1882

Natural desire gives you no right to any particular woman: that comes with love only ...

ibid.

Of all the cruel things in life, the cruellest, it may be, is the departure of all beauty from those who have been the desired mothers and mistresses of men in a former generation.

Memories & Portraits, 'Memoirs of himself'

It is easier to tell a falsehood than to pacify a discontented woman.

Fables and Other Stories and Fragments,
'When the devil was well'

... there is something more substantive about a woman than ever there can be about a man.

to Mrs Sitwell, Apr. 1876

I walk the streets smoking my pipe
And I love the dallying shopgirl
That leans with rounded stern to look at the fashions.

Poems, vol. 2, 'New poems'

A girl or two at play in a corner of waste-land
Tumbling and showing their legs and crying out to me
loosely.

ibid.

Marriage is a step so grave and decisive that it attracts light-headed, variable men by its very awfulness.

Virginibus Puerisque, pt. 1

... the man who should hold back from marriage is in the same case with him who runs away from battle.

ibid.

For marriage is like life in this – that it is a field of battle, and not a bed of roses.

ibid.

Even if we take matrimony at its lowest, even if we regard it as no more than a sort of friendship recognised by the police ... *ibid.*

Marriage is terrifying, but so is a cold and forlorn old age. *ibid.*

In marriage, a man becomes slack and selfish, and undergoes a fatty degeneration of his moral being.

ibid.

I suspect love is rather too violent a passion to make, in all cases, a good domestic sentiment.

ibid.

The best of men and the best of women may sometimes live together all their lives, and for want of some consent on fundamental questions, hold each other lost spirits to the end.

ibid.

... no woman should marry a teetotaller, or a man who does not smoke. *ibid.*

To dwell happily together, they should be versed in the niceties of the heart, and born with a faculty for willing compromise. *ibid.*

To marry is to domesticate the Recording Angel.

ibid., pt. 2

You may think you had a conscience, and believed in God: but what is a conscience to a wife?

ibid.

... there is probably no other act in a man's life so hot-headed and foolhardy as this one of marriage.

ibid.

Trusty, dusky, vivid, true,
With eyes of gold and bramble-dew,
Steel-true and blade-straight,
The great artificer
Made my mate.

Poems, vol. 1, 'Songs of travel'

I don't care so much for solitude as I used to: results, I suppose, of marriage.

to Charles Baxter, Dec. 1881

Marriage is one long conversation, chequered by disputes.

Memories & Portraits, 'Talk and talkers', pt. 2

Every man is bound to marry above him; if the woman's not the man's superior, I brand it as mere sensuality.

The Wrecker, ch. 3

Jack Sprat and his wife in the nursery rhyme, offer an ideal example of adaptation for co-existence.

Memories & Portraits, 'From his notebook'

No considerate man can approach marriage without deep concern.

Ethical Studies, 'Reflections and remarks on human life', pt. 10

Writers

[Of Shaw] It is horrid fun. All I ask is more of it ... tell me more of the inimitable author.

to William Archer, Winter 1888

[Of Shaw] 1 part Charles Reade; 1 part Henry James or some kindred author badly assimilated; $\frac{1}{2}$ part Disraeli (perhaps unconscious); $1\frac{1}{2}$ parts struggling, over-laid original talent; 1 part blooming, gaseous folly.

ibid.

What books Dickens could have written had he been permitted! Think of Thackeray as unfettered as Flaubert or Balzac! What books I might have written myself! But they give us a little box of toys, and say to us, 'You mustn't play with anything but these.'

An Intimate Portrait of RLS

Do you know who is my favourite author just now? How are the mighty fallen! Anthony Trollope.

to Mr & Mrs Thomas Stevenson, Feb. 1878

Browning made the verses
Your servant the critique.
Browning couldn't sing at all
I fancy I could speak.
Although his book was clever
(To give the deil his due)
I wasn't pleased with Browning's verse
Nor he with my review.   *Collected Poems*, 'Light verse'

[Of Balzac] He was a man who never found his method. An inarticulate Shakespeare, smothered under forcible-feeble detail.   to R.A.M. Stevenson, Oct. 1883

I mean to read Boswell now until the day I die

to Mrs Sitwell, July 1876

Byron not only wrote Don Juan; he called Joan of Arc 'a fanatical strumpet'. These are his words.

to W.E. Henley, Apr. 1882

Some like Poe
And others like Scott,
Some like Mrs Stowe;
Some not.   *A Child's Garden of Verses*

Virgil is one of the tops of human achievement.

to Sidney Colvin, Mar. 1886

[Of himself] I am pioching, like a madman, at my stories, and can make nothing of them; my simplicity is tame and dull – my passion tinsel, boyish, hysterical.

to Sidney Colvin, Feb. 1875

[Of Burns] I made a kind of chronological table of his various loves and lusts, and have been comparatively speechless ever since.

to Edmund Gosse, July 1879

[Of Burns] His humour comes from him in a stream so deep and easy that I will venture to call him the best of humorous poets.

Familiar Studies of Men & Books, 'Aspects of Burns'

Burns was so full of his identity that it breaks forth on every page.   *ibid.*

And one thing is certain, that no one can appreciate Whitman's excellences until he has grown accustomed to his faults.   *ibid.*, 'Walt Whitman'

Every one has been influenced by Wordsworth, and it is hard to tell precisely how.

Essays Literary & Critical, 'Books which have influenced me'

[Of Jules Verne] His characters being dolls, it is truly instructive to see how well he juggles with them. He has the knack of making stories to a nicety.

ibid., 'Jules Verne's stories'

[Of Jules Verne] These tales of his are not true, but they do not seem to fall altogether under the heading of impossible.

ibid.

Jules Verne careers on the paper with the most flagrant and detestable vivacity.

ibid.

[Of Thackeray] If Rawdon Crawley's blow were not delivered, Vanity Fair would cease to be a work of art.

Memories & Portraits, 'A gossip on romance'

Walter Scott is out and away the king of the romantics.

ibid.

[Of Scott] Of the pleasures of his art he tasted fully; but of its toils and vigils and distresses never man knew less. A great romantic – an idle child.

ibid.

[Of Swinburne] I could tell a lot of funny stories of the days when he was partial to the bottle, and I had rather not.

ibid., 'Memoirs of himself'

[Of Hazlitt] I could have thought he had been eavesdropping at the door of my heart, so entire was the coincidence between his writing and my thought.

Further Memories, 'A retrospect'

Chaucer, Spenser, Shakespeare, Milton, Pope, Wordsworth, Shelley – what a constellation of lordly words!

Virginibus Puerisque, 'Philosophy of nomenclature'

I am the last of Scotland's three Robbies, Robbie Burns, Robbie Fergusson, and Robbie Stevenson – and how hardly life treated them all, poor devils!

An Intimate Portrait of RLS

Youth & Age

For God's sake give me the young man who has brains enough to make a fool of himself!

Virginibus Puerisque, 'Crabbed age and youth'

All sorts of allowances are made for the illusions of youth; and none, or almost none, for the disenchantments of age.

ibid.

Old and young, we are all on our last cruise.

ibid.

It is as natural and as right for a young man to be imprudent and exaggerated, to live in swoops and circles, and beat about his cage like any other wild thing newly captured, as it is for old men to turn gray.

ibid.

A full, busy youth is your only prelude to a self-contained and independent age; and the muff inevitably develops into the bore.

ibid.

Youth is the time to go flashing from one end of the world to the other both in mind and body.

ibid.

When the old man waggles his head and says, 'Ah, so I thought when I was your age', he has proved the youth's case.

ibid.

To love playthings well as a child, to lead an adventurous and honourable youth and to settle, when the time arrives, into a green and smiling age is to be a good artist in life and deserve well of yourself and your neighbour.

ibid.

It is good to have been young in youth, and, as years go on, to grow older ...

ibid., Dedication

The best that is in us is better than we understand; for it is grounded beyond experience, and guides us, blindfold but safe, from one age on to another.

ibid.

Sing me a song of a lad that is gone,
Say, could that lad be I?
Merry of soul he sailed on a day
Over the sea to Skye.

Poems, vol. 1, 'Songs of travel'

We'll walk the woods no more
But stay beside the fire,
To weep for old desire
And things that are no more.

to Mrs Sitwell, Aug. 1875

To know what you like is the beginning of wisdom and of old age.

Essays Literary & Critical, 'Letter to a young gentleman'

Youth is wholly experimental.   *ibid.*

The best teachers are the aged.

Memories & Portraits, 'Talk and talkers', pt. 2

... memories are a fairy gift which cannot be worn out in using.   *ibid.*, 'Memoirs of an islet'

By the time a man gets well into his seventies, his continued existence is a mere miracle ...

Virginibus Puerisque, 'Aes triplex'

'Be ashamed of yourself,' said the Frog. 'When I was a Tadpole, I had no tail.'
'Just what I thought,' said the Tadpole. 'You never were a Tadpole.'

Fables and Other Stories and Fragments